Healing Splintered Souls

*Reshaping Sudanese America
Culture, Creed, Children*

Mohamed N. Bushara, PhD

Copyright © 2017 Mohamed N. Bushara
All rights reserved. No part of this publication may be reproduced, stored in a retrieval system, or transmitted in any form or by any means electronic, mechanical, photocopying, recording or otherwise, without the written permission of Mohamed N. Bushara.

The information provided within this book is for general informational purposes only. The methods described within this book are the author's personal thoughts. They are not intended to be a definitive set of instructions for all situations.

Although the author and publisher have made every effort to ensure that the information in this book is correct at the time of publication, the author and publisher do not assume and hereby disclaim any liability for any incomplete, erroneous or outdated information.

To protect the privacy of certain individuals the names and identifying details may have been changed.

Written by Mohamed N. Bushara with Kate E. Stephenson

CONTENTS

Acknowledgements 1
Author's Note 3
Introduction: Why Should I Care? 5
Chapter One: Sudanese Community Challenges 11
    Statistics: Sudanese in America 14
    Statistics: African Americans 19
    Uncontrollable Challenges 22
    Controllable Challenges 29
    Challenges Wrap-Up 33
Chapter Two: Responding to the Challenges 35
    Understanding the Numbers 36
    Responding to Uncontrollable Challenges 39
    Responding to Controllable Challenges 57
    Responding Wrap-Up 64
Chapter Three: Raising Children In Diaspora 65
    Childrearing Challenges 67
    Childrearing Comeback 75
    Rearing Wrap-Up 82
Conclusion: Removing the Splinter 83
    The Individual Soul 83
    The Soul of the People 84
Bibliography 87

Acknowledgements

I would like to thank the Sudanese American Medical Association (SAMA) for sharing their Chicago Health Fair study and its findings, and for generously giving permission to share them with you in this publication. These kinds of studies are too few; it is my hope that in the years to come more information will become available about the migrant Sudanese diaspora around the world. SAMA's work is invaluable and a vital benefit both in the United States and in Sudan.

I would also like to thank Kate Stephenson, my editor, for her assistance throughout this process. Her deep research skills have helped to ground my ideas and beliefs in established facts and statistical information. Her writing is brilliant, and I am honored to have worked with her.

Last but certainly not least, I would like to thank my family who are the inspiration for this book. Thank you for your love and support.

Author's Note

My goal in writing this book is to provide a resource to my fellow Sudanese immigrants. I want to help my community acclimate and integrate into American life. When I left my homeland, Sudan was still one nation. In 2011, to my deep sorrow, my countrymen split the state in two. After years of inequality, inequity, and in-fighting between factions, Sudan is now North and South. While I wish to speak to all Sudanese here, I understand that the separation is far deeper than political differences. Many South Sudanese are of Christian and animist faiths, while North Sudanese are majority Muslim. By birth and custom I would now be considered North Sudanese. Because this book is based greatly on my own experiences, I have directed this conversation primarily toward other North Sudanese.

I cannot speak to what it is like to be a Christian or an animist in a new nation, or in this Western context. Likewise, I cannot speak to being a woman or even a child in this long journey. But I can speak to what I have experienced and observed. As a father, a black man, a scholar, a professional, a traveler and a Muslim, I have seen many things. I do believe that all Sudanese immigrants, as well as immigrants from other parts of Africa and the diaspora will find benefit in this book. Many of the themes that are discussed here are common for all strangers in a new land.

I also fully believe that the Sudanese, regardless of current circumstances, have a common world view and understanding of our own culture and customs. Whether North, South, or others in the wider continent of Africa, we have experienced the same whitewashing of our history, of our blackness, of our heritage. We share a defined past, and are linked in the struggle for a better future.

So when I say Sudanese, my point of view stems from Sudan and looks over the world, seeing my brothers and sisters across the globe—all of us experiencing the same identity split and trying to heal.

INTRODUCTION

WHY SHOULD I CARE?

Wherever you go, you take yourself with you.

That statement may seem obvious, but it's often the common sense things that escape our notice. As a Sudanese immigrant to the United States, and many places before that, this is a truth that I have come to know and understand intimately. But it is so easy to forget. Wherever any individual travels, they take their knowledge, experience, skills and talents with them. They also take their prejudices, preconceived notions, and ill-informed opinions. In our journeys, we bring with us both the good and the bad, the best of us and the worst.

You say, so what? How is this relevant to me?

There are two things that are generally true for every immigrant: 1. You are leaving your home—all that is familiar to you. 2. You are going to a new place—one you hope will be better than where you left. Here is how it is relevant: If you know little about your destination, you may not be able to find the better life you hope for. And more importantly, if you bring all your baggage and dirt with you, you will simply recreate your old problems in your new home.

In order to make a new start, you just might have to make a new YOU.

What worked in a prior place may not work in the new one. The skills you had before may not benefit you now. The behaviors that helped you create community before, may isolate you today. The attitudes that got you through past crises may not bring you long-term success.

Sudanese immigrants and refugees have sought advice from religious leaders and elders on how to navigate their new reality. This book is a response to my fellow community members who ask, "How do people do it? How do they become successful in this new place?" Working class parents especially have great concerns. They ask: How do I handle my children growing up in this culture? How do I keep my kids out of trouble? Truancy from school, criminal behavior, and outright disrespect toward parents—these are problems that plague our ranks. We are splintered between our old selves and our new circumstances. The Sudan that many of us grew up in is gone, and we have not yet figured out what it means to be American.

How do you find success in such confusion?

The answer is simple, although not easy.

Integration.

I worked with my wife, my children, my community to integrate into this new home we have created together in the United States. Notice, I didn't say *assimilate*. I have in no way given up the proud Sudanese man I was raised to be. Instead I have expanded, grown into a greater version of myself—not because I have become American but because I have adopted the best of what America has to offer and retained the best of my Sudanese roots. I have become a compound, taking advantage of the opportunities here that I could not have in Sudan and enriching this new home with the warmth, hospitality, intelligence and fortitude instilled in me at birth.

I am not an exception. I believe that we can support each other in creating happier, healthier families wherever we choose to live. But we need to acknowledge some difficult truths, let go of some unproductive baggage, and unite as a community to be successful.

When I say integration, I do not mean just integrating as new Americans, but as a united Sudanese community. I want to build bridges among all Sudanese from pre-separation days, but the reality is that South and North Sudanese are isolating themselves. We have established small enclaves that do not communicate with each other. But how far will separation take us? I am a fierce proponent of having a unified Sudan again. We must resolve this separationist hysteria and we must do it together.

The pages that follow will explain some of the root causes of these problems, as well as provide some straightforward strategies to address them. In understanding how to protect and bring profit to our children, we have to first turn inward and look at ourselves as parents. We must begin to make major changes within *ourselves* before demanding change from our families.

First, we must strive to establish a solid spiritual base and positive social network to help us maintain a net positive perspective. This foundation will support and uplift the spirit, injecting a forward-looking optimism that can be transferred to our families. Where there is hope there is opportunity. In this land, there is opportunity everywhere you look, but often our perceptions keep us from gaining their full benefit.

Then, we must seek ways to integrate with the local community. Holding on to the past will only cripple us; we must learn to engage where we are and claim this place as our home. Once, we as parents have accomplished these things, we must foster our children's involvement in the activities that bind the community. When our children feel supported, included and engaged they will be less susceptible to negative influences.

We therefore must shift our model of life adapted to overcome the events and problems we faced in Sudan, and begin to create a new narrative of culture here in the USA. When we pay close attention to what is happening around us, we can educate ourselves such that we can make informed choices in our new homeland. There are healthy methods to eliminate misalignment with Western culture. Those points of cultural intersection will reveal opportunities to expand our own understandings and those of our new neighbors (Figure 1).

We are more than refugees. We are more than immigrants. We are more than poverty stricken. We are more than un- and underemployed. We are more than welfare recipients. We are more than our skin color. We are not statistics.

We must strive to become long-term society planners, fostering empathy, respect, and love for other Sudanese regardless of tribe, skin shade or hair length AND for our new American neighbors with whom we share a similar ignorance that can be cured with information.

We start here.

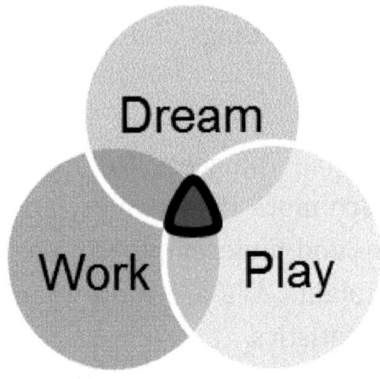

Figure 1. Focus: Choice alignment with objectives of western life

CHAPTER ONE

SUDANESE COMMUNITY CHALLENGES

We face so many challenges as migrants to the United States. Some of these challenges we have no control over and we have no means of changing. We have little choice but to adapt to these new circumstances. Other challenges we have a great deal of control over. Where we can do something about potential difficulties, we must. To allow issues that are in our control to define our future is a fool's errand. Even through unimaginable hardship, our resilience and unbreakable cultural heritage has proven that we are not fools.

Whatever challenges we face here are far less destructive to the human spirit than what we have escaped in Sudan—a systematic, government-supported collage of discriminatory practices based on skin color, ideology, tribe and culture. Yes, we will find prejudice and discrimination here, but never to the extent of that in our motherland (Figure 2). The US has seen a strong uptick in problems driven by bias in the past few years. Transitioning from the nation's first black president to the nation's first president openly supported by White Nationalists has created many tensions. Even with that, the laws of this land, the widespread belief in equality and justice, and a culture that supports human rights and dignity are still the norms here.

There are three primary issues that we cannot escape or deny in coming to America: 1) Whether we like it or not, we Sudanese are black; 2) by and large, we are Muslims, which is complicated by international issues and sensationalist news coverage and media; and finally, 3) we are overwhelmingly poor. These are the greatest stressors that may affect our successful entry into this new world. There is an inherit influx of stress and tension associated with these factors. On top of that, there is the reality of being in a new place with new social expectations, cultural expressions, laws and procedures. Small daily things that you have never encountered before... Missing the creature comforts of home that you simply cannot find here... all of this will have a profound effect on our physical, mental and spiritual health.

Depending on the choices we make and the actions we take, we can alter the outcome of a perceived challenge or even erase it completely. Armed with more information, we can make smarter choices and take positive action. Statistics have a way of providing snapshots of information. So, let's start with a few numbers to consider.

Figure 2. Comparison of burdens on our shoulders in US and Sudan

STATISTICS: SUDANESE IN AMERICA

Two surveys were conducted on representative populations of Sudanese refugees and immigrants: one set living in Denver, Colorado, the other in Chicago, Illinois.

The fundamental basis of the Denver survey was to establish ground-truth information from the community to ascertain the level of education, health, and integration problems they encounter. The survey also highlighted persistent gaps in basic quality of life on all fronts: education, employment, health and overall resettlement.

The Chicago study was conducted at a health fair in 2013. The resulting paper states: "Chicago is home to a large Sudanese population predominantly recent immigrants. There is anecdotal evidence that they predominantly have poor access to health care and poor health status." The health fair was established to help address these issues. To the 49 participants (10 female and 39 male), the fair provided body mass index (BMI), blood pressure (BP), total cholesterol, and blood sugar measurement. Volunteers passed out specially designed healthy life style brochures in Arabic. Board Certified doctors gave individualized health and wellness advice, with referral to Emergency Room/Urgent Care/ Primary Care as needed for those with abnormal results.

The results of the survey and additional research paint a challenging picture:

Family

Most adults were married with children.

Language

For most Sudanese, Arabic is the first language, with English as a less proficient second language.

Education

95% of refugee adults 18 years of age or older, did not have a high school diploma; average level of education: 7th grade.

85% of refugees were not currently enrolled in school, but many expressed a strong desire to do so if given the means and opportunity.

Employment

40% unemployment among recently arrived refugees.

Income

Median income for refugees: less than $20,000 per year per household ($43,800 median for foreign-born blacks (pew).

MORTALITY AND HEALTH

In Chicago:
The participants were relatively healthy 68% showing no major health conditions: 14% had hypertension, 7% diabetes, 10% both hypertension and diabetes, and 2% with hepatitis B.

59% had NO health insurance.

21% hadn't seen a doctor in 2 or more years.

71% of those over age 50 had never had a colonoscopy, a major cancer screening procedure for both men and women.

75% of women over age 50 had never had a mammogram, a major cancer screening procedure.

82.5% were considered overweight; 30.5% were considered obese.

28.5% were prehypertensive.

In Sudan:
Death rate is 7.3 per 1,000. Life expectancy is 64.4 years.

LIVING CONDITIONS

No health insurance except for a handful rich and those affiliated with the government.

No colonoscopy cancer screening of those over age 50, both men and women. It is just too expensive.

No mammogram major cancer screening procedure until the disease occurs.

Most people are suffering from poor nutrition, hypertension and diabetes.

In addition to the education and economic concerns, this research shows that Sudanese struggle to get good medical attention for themselves and their families. This stems from lack of quality insurance or any insurance at all, as a result of under- and unemployment.

Statistics: African Americans

As first generation migrants, many of us do not fall into these statistical populations. However the information here is important to understand how others—people who do not know who we are or our own customs—may view us simply because we resemble in skin color these populations. It is also good to understand the pitfalls that await us in "easy" assimilation.

Family (as of 2015)

70% of new mothers are single or unwed

67% of children live in a single-mother household

Education (as of 2015)

6.5% drop out of high school; only 76.4% graduate on time

84.7% of blacks over age 25 have high school equivalency

22.5% have bachelor's degree (national average, 32.5%)

Income (as of 2015)

$36,544 median income (national median, $55,775)

25.4% below poverty level

INCARCERATION AND CRIME

Approximately 50% of murder victims are black, although blacks make up only 13.3% of the population

83% of black murders are perpetrated by another black person

> BUT the number of blacks being killed by blacks is going down, while whites killed by whites is going up at a faster rate—this is never discussed

Incarcerated 5 times the rate of whites

Imprisonment of *women* is twice that of white women

2.3 million, 34% of the total 6.8 million correctional population

32% of all children arrested, 42% of children detained

52% of children whose cases are sent to adult criminal court

African Americans and Hispanics make up 32% of US population but 56% of all incarcerated people

HEALTH & MORTALITY

Death rate is 7.35 per 1,000.

Life expectancy is 4 years less than whites as of 2015, but this disparity has dropped by 25% in the last 16 years

Leading causes of death: Heart Disease, Cancer, Stroke

> These are aggravated by high incidence of:
> Obesity — 37.6% men; 56.9% women
> Hypertension — 40.9% men: 44.8% women, and
> Smoking — 21.6% men; 14.1% women

Blacks suffer from racial bias and discrimination in healthcare, from greater wait times to doctor's providing less pain management and performing unnecessary or unequal procedures.

A history of inequality and injustice has produced a political, economic and social playing field that is uneven. Voting disenfranchisement, zoning, industrial pollution, natural disasters, health care access and other issues create the poor living conditions of many black neighborhoods, both rural and urban. The increasing divide between middle class and lower class also increases the gap in information and resource access for those who most need it.

These are sad numbers, to be sure. There is no getting around it. Many of us fleeing Sudan under refugee status, or entering this country under diversity visas, have left in order to find better opportunities. We find ourselves entering this society under an umbrella "black" that has systematically been oppressed, repressed and depressed for centuries. This is the truth. But it is not the end of the story. Today we have advantages that were not available as recently as 20 years ago. The gaps are closing at ever increasing rates. We are living in the best American generation and we have a great deal to contribute.

Let's look more closely at the challenges, those we can control and those we cannot.

Uncontrollable Challenges

When we say uncontrollable here, we mean circumstances that have existed well before our migration to the US that will extend for some time after. This is not to say that these are issues that cannot be addressed, handled, and overcome. Rather, these are issues that almost all of us will have to deal with at some point or another. There is very little you can do to escape these challenges but there is much you can do to successfully face them in a positive spirit with a positive outcome.

History

We cannot escape that we have emigrated from a war-torn, underdeveloped country that has been pilfered by European and Arab governments alike. This is the history of our country. While we were not bought and sold in the transatlantic slave trade, we have our own history of slavery and servitude. In modern times, we have been deemed second class citizens. Even as we have adopted an Arab identity, we have never been accepted in Middle Eastern Arab countries as anything but black. This schism in our realities has led to infighting, division, and internal power struggles for the barest of scraps.

This is the history and mentality with which we come to the US, but it does not need to be our future. There are opportunities here that were out of most of our grasp in Sudan, regardless of self-classifications. Arab or black, Muslim, Christian or animist—we have all come here for a better life. But if we live by the same mindset as in Sudan we will shackle ourselves to the same unnecessary hardships.

Race

We are no strangers to colorism, tribalism and prejudice. But in Sudan these problems are nuanced in different ways than the racism found in the United

States. While we may consider ourselves Arab first and black second (if at all), in the United States, we will be seen in relation to our skin color. Not our tribe, not our language, not our religion first. And none of those aspects will necessarily gain us any benefit. The history of race in the United States is complex but in some ways quite simple. One drop of African blood has historically categorized one forever as black. This is underscored by a cultural gaze that classifies all of a darker hue as black.

However we see ourselves, Americans will see us as black. This is as American as apple pie.

Economics

Many of us migrate to the US with very little money. That is a fact of refugee status. And those of us with some means and education may find that those resources do not carry us as far as we might expect in this land. We general have not had opportunities within our war-torn country to create economic gains, and so we cannot condemn ourselves because of this unfortunate situation. It is a challenge to create opportunities for ourselves. Lack of education drastically limits work options. In addition, there is a real racial gap for income in the US; on average, blacks do not make as much money as whites, simply by virtue of being black. According to a 2017 study conducted by the Institute on Assets and Social Policy, the average wealth of whites with some college education was $79,600, as compared to blacks with some college at $11,100. Big difference. This study showed that there are many reasons for this gap. The most obvious is being that those with wealth can more easily create more wealth. Starting from nothing, it is difficult to make something—but not impossible. We cannot change that we come here poor and black, but we can work our way out of poverty, through education, hard work, and personal betterment.

LOCALITY

Often your zip code, the neighborhood in which you live, determines the quality and length of your families' life. Access to services, schools, police, health care, financial products, etc., are closely linked to this information. Unfortunately, we do not always have control over where we are relocated through programs, or where we can afford to live upon gaining entry to the US. Poor and predominantly minority residential areas receive less attention from the city, state and federal policy makers compared to suburban areas and affluent neighborhoods. While this may be unavoidable in the early days of migration, there are many ways to alleviate some of the hardships associated with locality.

Healthcare

Immigration is emotionally, mentally and physically stressful. Language, economic and social barriers often leave us without the healthcare access that is necessary to thrive. This is especially true when it comes to prenatal and infant care, where we have seen the effects evidenced in frequent miscarriages and premature pregnancies (Denver study).

Like other blacks in the country, the Sudanese community will be victims of implicit racial medicine in hospitals and clinics as indicated above no matter how much money we make. Racial bias cuts across all economic levels. These biases in large part are based on ideas instilled by renowned plantation physicians like Dr. James Marion Sims (1813–1883) who subscribed to a now commonly held belief that *"Africans had a specific physiological tolerance for pain, unknown by whites."* He never felt the need to anesthetize his black patients in Montgomery, Alabama. From prenatal care through elder care, we must be vigilant to become knowledgeable about our health, common diseases, expectations of healthcare and insurance, and be vocal advocates for our own health.

Mortality

According to recent statistics, a black person dies

every 7 minutes, which is over 205 every day. Blacks in the US are expected to die an average of 3.5 years earlier than their white counterparts. We are at higher risk from every cause of death. This stems from ingrained prejudicial healthcare practices as well as culture. In addition, hygiene, disease and lack of early life healthcare prior to immigration, may contribute to increased death risk within our populations. A further extension, diet plays a large part in health. It has been shown that the traditional African diet is healthier for those of African descent, however, the American diet, heavy on carbohydrates and processed sugars, has trickled into many of our homes as these foods are cheap and easily accessible. These are not easily overcome, but in addressing the previous challenges, life expectancy does not have to be limited.

Policing & Justice System

The community will be victim to racial profiling and police focus. Profiling relies on skin color and cultural markers. As black Muslims we are at even greater risk in this political environment. As a black person, you are more susceptible to police brutality and ill-treatment even if you are the victim of a crime. Once within the system, without money to engage personal legal assistance, we are left to the overworked, underpaid legal aid workers. These defense lawyers may not see you as an individual but as one of hundreds of case numbers, and may be less motivated to present a quality defense due to personal preconceptions and professional pressures. While recent studies have found that immigrants as a whole statistically commit fewer crimes, as a black person you are more likely to encounter a legal problem within your lifetime than other counterparts. We must be aware and be prepared. We may not be able to control this challenge but we can learn for ourselves and teach our children how to address police officers. We can learn about our own local, state and federal laws and the rights they do and do *not* guarantee. We can work to gather correct information and not act on emotions or instinct alone.

Culture Clash

The United States was founded on the premise of separation of church and state (religion and the legal system), and freedom of religion is written into the US Constitution. However, the majority of the country still identifies as Christian. Very few people have met people of other religions. Even though Islam is the second largest religion in the world, Muslims are still a small minority here. Muslims make up only about 1% of the US population. 3.3 million sounds like a lot of people—and it is—but in a country of more than

300 million we remain a marginal and marginalized people.

It is a reality that the majority of Americans will not understand our religion or our customs. Given recent media, it is almost inevitable that our religion and customs may scare ignorant and ill-informed Americans. In recent years, the word "terrorist" has become synonymous with "Muslim". We know this to be a falsehood. It is difficult—but not impossible—to combat these misconceptions.

Controllable Challenges

Here when we say controllable challenge, what we mean is the attitudes, information and inclination we adopt in addressing life situations. These are not the challenges that other circumstances dictate but rather the individual steps we take to improve our lives and help our children succeed and prosper.

Communication

Poor communication skills due to a language barrier will exacerbate ill-treatment of others toward you. Improvement in communication skills leads to better chances of being hired to good employment. It may not be fair, but people treat you better when they can understand you. While you may not lose your accent, people will respect you for your effort to speak correctly and make your point eagerly.

It is important to present ideas in acceptable ways to have maximum impact. Being mindful of how you say things and in what tone can make a big difference in how you are received.

The majority of communication is nonverbal. It's not what you say that speaks the loudest. How you look, how you present yourself to the world will announce who you are before you ever open your mouth. Your level of cleanness, the style of your wardrobe and hair, your body language and demeanor are all ways that you communicate to those around you.

ATTITUDE

Tribalism and prejudice have followed us from Sudan to the US. Everyone gets into their tribal tent and does not bother with others, even though we are all Sudanese. There is generally lack of trust between various tribes. There are historical reasons for these conflicts. The ethnic groupings and tribalism that caused civil wars and genocides in Sudan are still present in communities here in the US. We have been unable to forget what happened to our families and villages.

But we must ask ourselves: do those historical reasons serve us in these new circumstances?

Many hold on to a grudge without even remembering how the grudge began. In a new place where we are so few, those old disputes will cause us nothing more than further separation and self-segregation.

We have the ability to say "enough."

Where will exclusionary practices get us? Holding on to the negativity of a bygone era will only bring pessimism into our new situation. We have left Sudan for a reason—better opportunity. We must adopt an attitude worthy of inviting that opportunity in.

Adopting a community attitude that embraces fellow Sudanese in the US, as well as reaches out to embrace other American populations, we will become more successful. Some of us may be lucky enough to find communities that wholeheartedly embrace us, but we must be ready to embrace others and resist the inclination to become isolated and exclusionary.

Program Dependence

The idea of welfare is seductive. Free money from a government that takes care of its people—it sounds like the miracle for which you have been looking. It is NOT. There are visible and invisible strings attached to these government "handouts".

First, you must understand it is not a foregone conclusion that you will qualify for welfare programs and continue on them forever. Second, even if you could, this is in fact a handicap and contrary to the customs and values that were instilled in us.

Like all things associated with all governments, there is a lot of red tape involved. Once you qualify for programs you must continue to qualify for them. That is the trap. Free government discourages those under the welfare system to break the poverty ceiling. While programs that provide seemingly free money seem amazing, they will never provide enough. You must continue to be poor in order to continue to get the meager benefits. And they are meager in comparison to what you will find when you start to earn good money. Although many believe that this is a good way of milking the government, it is a killing instrument of individual aspirations and a roadblock to upward social mobility (Figure 3).

For new immigrants and refugee arrivals, assistance may help you get your feet on the ground, but seek opportunities to get out of it as soon as possible.

Steady employment/higher wages
Safer environment/more opportunities
Better schools, improved education
Unified, happier families
Higher self esteem and confidence

Government Assistance/Welfare
Low income & Poor Job Prospects
Poverty-stricken neighborhoods
Underperforming schools
Broken Families

Figure 3. We need to get out of welfare system

CHALLENGES WRAP-UP

While there are many challenges ahead, both controllable and uncontrollable, specific to Sudanese immigrants and those generally applicable to blacks in the US, there is great hope to overcome all of these real and potential obstacles. We explore how in the next chapter.

CHAPTER TWO

RESPONDING TO THE CHALLENGES

Short-term hyper-reactionary methods or the "sandbag strategy" is a shortsighted life strategy. Short-term solutions and quick fixes are band-aids on gaping wounds—they will do little in the long run to help us reach our individual and collective goals. Working towards lasting long-term solutions may take longer to achieve—maybe longer than we will live to see ourselves—but our families will reap the rewards.

We need to become long term thinkers (Long-termism). Instead of planning for today and tomorrow, we need to plan for next year and the next decade, and farther into the future.

We must stop using hyper-reactionary measures, only reacting to the immediate crisis without thinking about life beyond. Once we have weathered the immediate storm, then what?

First let's deal with these statistics.

Understanding the Numbers

We have some knowledge of our own histories within our mother country, but even there our understanding is clouded by opinion, government propaganda, a biased educational system, and the vestiges of colonial rules. We must keep in mind that the US has its own histories masked by similar means. The history of people of color in America is told quite often through the eyes of her colonists, not through the eyes of the indigenous peoples who were here first or the millions of people brought here through bondage and servitude (of many different colors).

This obscured history sheds light on the statistics of African Americans discussed above, much the same way as the history that we know can explain ours. It is certainly not the truth that many of us only desire a secondary school education. If given a choice most of us would likely have college degrees, not just high school diplomas (although we would happily take that). With the opportunities we find here in this country many of us will obtain our diplomas and higher education degrees. It is the lack of such opportunity that explains the statistical data for black Americans. The same lack of education that leads to under employment and welfare dependence for us, affects the greater black American population, leading to a higher percentage of single female mothers and high incarceration, and lower mortality rates. This is a domino effect. One that African Americans have been struggling to overcome for centuries.

We learned about slavery in America on our own—the pop culture version. When I dug deeper to educate myself on the history of black people in this country, I was overwhelmed with emotions. I began to realize the extent of what enslaved black Africans suffered before and after the American Civil War to make way for us all to be here today.

Their first arrival to the North American colony of Jamestown, Virginia, was in 1619, to aid in the production of such lucrative crops as tobacco and cotton. From the start of the Civil War in 1861 until the emergence of the Civil Rights Movement in the 1960s, blacks were brutalized and suppressed through Jim Crow laws and other government sanctioned and legislated measures. Of particular significance is the inhumane way black people were experimented on and abused by the likes of Dr. Sims and others to do research to improve the lives of white people (See Harriet A. Washington's book *Medical Apartheid: The Dark History of Medical Experimentation on Black Americans from Colonial Times to the Present*).

Yes, we believe we are different from those who were enslaved in this country, but in reality we are not. While our ancestors were not involved in the

Transatlantic Slave Trade as either business partners or chattel, we have survived our own nightmares and inequality. No we were not slaves in the American sense, but we have known what it is like not to be free. Our own statistical information proves that.

It is the struggle of African Americans that has opened the doors to the opportunity that we now enjoy. Affirmative action, civil rights, human rights, equal education rights—these have all been fought for through generations of activists who dedicated and lost their lives to these causes. It is easy to turn your nose up at a population defined by the numbers above if you do not understand the circumstances behind them. Coming from a place of struggle and oppression, we should have more empathy, compassion and solidarity for our black brothers and sisters. And understand none of us are numbers.

Responding to Uncontrollable Challenges

Embrace Blackness

As a community, we must step up and embrace the fact that *we are black people.* The sooner we embrace our black African identity the better for our community and children. The race/ethnic identity classification in this country does not cater to blacks of Sudanese origin as a separate group of blacks (Figure 4). Others will not recognize you as a different class of black. To disassociate yourself from black Americans and the history of slavery is to divorce yourself from a rich culture. The continuous struggle of blacks in this country paved the way for other Africans to migrate here and reap the opportunities we are now afforded.

Professor Henry Louis "Skip" Gates Jr. of Harvard University visited East Africa taking a journey from Egypt in the north to Tanzania in the easternmost. According to the professor, his trip was a very disappointing experience. In his video he tacitly illustrates that to be identified as black is something that all run away from. As Prof. Skip found out, Africans in the

RACE/ETHNIC IDENTIFICATION – PLEASE CHECK ALL THAT APPLY	
☐ **Hispanic or Latino** (A person of Cuban, Mexican, Puerto Rican, South or Central American, or other Spanish culture or origin, regardless of race.)	☐ **Native Hawaiian or other Pacific Islander** (A person having origins in the original peoples of Hawaii, Guam, Samoa, or other Pacific Islands.)
☐ **American Indian or Alaska Native** (A person having origins in any of the original peoples of North or South America, including Central America, and who maintains tribal affiliations or community attachment.)	☒ **Black or African American** (A person having origins in any of the black racial groups of Africa.)
☐ **Asian** (A person having origin in any of the original peoples of the Far East, Southeast Asia, or the Indian subcontinent including, for example, Cambodia, China, India, Japan, Korea, Malaysia, Pakistan, the Philippine Islands, Thailand, and Vietnam.)	☐ **White/Caucasian** (A person having origins in any of the original peoples of Europe, the Middle East, or North Africa.)

Figure 4. Race/ethnic identity classification in US

eastern section of Africa who are born and raised on the Island of Zanzibar say they are Persians; those in Tanzania say they are Arabs from the Arabian subcontinent. He cites how ancient and modern Egyptians tried to erase traces and accomplishments of black Africans such as Baankhy and Hatshepsut the black king and queen and replace them with Arab-derived achievements. Even Nubians in northern Sudan vehemently disassociate themselves from the label "black". The Nubians portray themselves as the masters of black Africans, claiming an Arab ancestry from tribes in the Kingdom of Saudi Arabia (KSA) and other Middle Eastern countries, even though they bare black skin.

The truth is no one wants to be black.

There is a centuries old belief that lighter skin is more beautiful and darker skin is ugly. We have taught our children this nonsense, teaching them that blackness is worthless. We can see this phenomenon all over the world particularly in countries that were colonized by Europeans. A noted exception is Ethiopia which was not colonized by whites, defeating the Italians in the late 19th century. In Ethiopia, the base of beauty and elegance is black and the darker the skin is, the more beautiful the person. Dark skinned Ethiopians are considered the offspring of kings and rulers. Whereas light skinned people are perceived to be poor workers whose skin got flushed by the heat of the sun and the harsh outdoor weather. But they have it wrong too. There is no evidence to suggest that color correlates with intellect or beauty.

But we have internalized the association between dark skin and slavery, light skin and freedom. Dr. M. Jalal Hashim speaks of this in his article "The Arabization of Sudan":

> *The Paradox of the Black Arab who is Anti-Black*
>
> *Thenceforward the Arabized Africans of middle Sudan will pose as non-black Arabs. Intermarriage with light-skinned people would be consciously sought as a process of cleansing blood from blackness. A long process of identity change has begun; in order to have access to power and to be at least accepted as free humans, African people tended to drop both their identities and languages and replace them with Arabic language and Arab identity. The first step in playing that game is to overtly deplore the blacks and dub them as slaves while being themselves black...*
>
> *This ideology of alienation has prevailed for the last five centuries up to the moment. It has been consolidated by successive political regimes – whether under the Turco-Egyptian or*

> Egyptian-British or national rule. It finds its roots in the vice of slavery. ... By sublimating the Arab as their model through this erroneous and confused concept of race, the Arabized people of Sudan have made themselves permanent second-class Arabs. The consequences of this do not only affect them, but also their whole country, now split up between Arabism and Africanism. It has never dawned on them that speaking a language does not necessarily equate becoming of the nationality bearing that language. In fact the so-called Arabs in Sudan comprise different peoples with different cultures but one language: they are Arabophone. The Sudanese people are Arabophone Africans just as there are Francophone and Anglophone Africans.

We describe ourselves as Afro-Arabians to distinguish ourselves from other black Africans. No one is teaching anything about slavery in the Sudanese curriculum, we have not examined our own history. We commonly point fingers referencing in discussions about what happened "over there" but not in Sudan. And yet, our history is still there if we wish to look. We have collectively thought of ourselves as better than our South Sudanese cousins—made them enemies because of their even darker skin tones and

Christian religion. What caused the south to split from Sudan was a form of slavery in treating South Sudanese people as an underclass. There are systematic policies and practices in the country that work against African-looking people, enslaving minds if not bodies. What we failed to realize is that in comparison to Middle East Arabs and whites, *we* are the African-looking people. We have been led to believe in falsehoods to protect the wealthy and their wealth. But do these policies help us?

It is hard to ignore our blackness, especially when confronted by a new culture that does not differentiate between Arabic-speaking, French-speaking, English-speaking, or other speaking blacks. Neither our language nor our religion will distinguish us from other blacks in the United States. We are viewed the same way in the eyes of the law and by the majority of the people. The only thing that will distinguish us is what we do in our black skin. But we will always still be wearing it. Therefore, we must acknowledge our race and work to project the goodness of the Sudanese identity and culture through our behavior, manners and demeanor.

RETHINK BLACK AMERICAN STEREOTYPES

We have a complicated history in Sudan. The United States has a complicated history of its own. We will be lumped into community with those who look most like us in the US by default. Yet we will not know each other or each other's struggles. The benefits of overcoming this ignorance may not be evident at first. It is difficult to see beyond stereotypes. As much as we *think* we know about black Americans, they have just as many misconceptions about us. These divisions only serve to weaken us on a local and on an international level.

In the 1970s through the 1990s there was a strong resurgence of Afrocentricity among black Americans. Many were searching for ways to reconnect with their lost African roots—to find out who they really were before the bondage of slavery or the displacement of wars. This has since been replaced by a cool period, partially generated by a lack of hospitality extended to them by their African cousins.

We have been conditioned by media to think of African Americans as inferior. News coverage focuses on killings, criminality and misdeeds. Black people are painted as savage, uncivilized menaces to society. And many of us have fallen for it. We see a lack of education, a concentration of black Americans in poverty-stricken areas, and we witness the misdirected rage of blacks as they protest. And we judge them. We judge them harshly. We are told it is right for us to judge them. That they should be seen as second-rate in comparison with our better manners, greater intellects, and trained civility. Yet we know that in Sudan we also are judged. We know that our war-torn country has seen many setbacks because of the isolation of many for the benefit of the few. We know how inequitably and unjustly the ruling class lords their riches and rights over the so-called underclasses. But we have not always applied this knowledge to the inhabitants of our new surroundings.

Just like we don't have a full understanding of the black community in the US, generally speaking, they have absolutely no idea who we are or what we have survived. You will find that generally Americans have a very insular understanding of the world. Add to that poor education and lack of access to travel. Many black Americans will not know where Sudan is or what is going on there. They may have heard of Darfur, but they may not even realize that it is a region in Sudan. Because Sudan has not received much news coverage lately, they may not even understand that our country has gone through a civil war and is now officially divided. And honestly, they may not care.

In many areas, black Americans are fighting their own wars every day. While the matters of Sudan may never have any real effect on Americans, the plight of African Americans will have a very real effect on us. The way we judge black Americans today will be the way others will judge our children tomorrow—if our children survive. Police bullets do not discriminate based on country of origin. Poverty does not discriminate based on language spoken or religious beliefs. The healthcare system is not color blind but it does not differentiate between shades of brown. We need to understand who African Americans are in order to understand what it means to be black in the United States.

We can start here: We do not respond positively to those who judge us. Therefore we should not expect a warm reception from those who feel judged by us. (Oscar Johnson looks at the ways in which Africans and US blacks view each other with judgmental puzzlement in his paper "Chilly Coexistence: Africans and African Americans in the Bronx".)

We must make an effort to abandon our preconceptions. If we look at the communities around us we will find many people who do not fit into these stereotypes. If we look deeper into why these stereotypes exist, we may find a commonality that shocks us. In many ways we are experiencing two sides of the same coin. And until we really look at each other for who we are and not who colonization has defined us as, or how the news would characterize us, or through the limitations of our bank accounts, education and opportunities — only then will we be able to see.

We cannot expect a warm welcome because they do not know us any more than we know them. But we can rely on a basic human truth that when treated with respect, most often people respond with respect. It is not a requirement to make friends with US blacks. But it just might be a benefit.

GROW YOUR FINANCIAL PROSPECTS

Economics are so often linked to education. It is simple: those with access to education are better equipped to excel in the work force. Here are some basic truths:

- → Blacks are as intelligent as anybody else.
- → Skin color and ethnicity have nothing to do with IQ scores or predicted success.

There are hundreds, perhaps thousands, of books written to make you and others think that we are inferior. It is nothing but propaganda to make the colonists feel better about themselves. Those who seek to use us for our resources but never compensate us—they are the only ones who benefit from these lies. People like Rush Limbaugh and other right-wing media, with their "conservative" rhetoric, extol the virtues of whiteness and the evils of liberal policies, but they are nothing but bullies. They boost themselves by stepping on and over people like us. We do not need to buy into their nonsense.

Numerous studies have shown that standardized tests (SAT, FRE, ACT) are not an accurate measurement of student abilities, knowledge or IQ. These tests are culturally biased and prove only that students know how to take standardized tests. Many schools are slowly but surely doing away with these inaccurate tools. Racial gaps in test results have been clearly linked to economic conditions, schooling, health and nutrition—not intelligence! When you are hungry, haven't slept well, are suffering from chronic diseases like asthma, and your family and school are both too poor to afford new text books and effective teachers—standardized test scores will obviously suffer. When inner-city black children were adopted by affluent white families, they performed equal to or *better* than their white counterparts in arithmetic and fast memory tests. There are greater differences between individuals than between ethnic groups. The allusion that ethnicity or racial IQ differences are genetically based no longer stands. This is not a racial or an intellectual condition—this is a socioeconomic condition.

When you understand and accept that you are just as capable and smart as anyone else, things change. The world becomes bigger and the opportunities become more apparent. We are in a position to assist each other in identifying and taking advantage of the opportunities that exist, even for the poorest of us. It is a challenge—but we are used to those. We have lived hard lives already. These are small changes we can make to live more fully into the American dream that we came here to find.

With better education come better job opportunities. These are not guaranteed, but more doors open with greater education. Starting with obtaining your high school equivalency or GED is the best first step. There are free GED courses online and in person; the full test is about $150—a large sum, but a small price to pay when you are twice as likely to get a job and will earn on average $10,000 more per year. There may also be community resources in your area that may help. Check your local library, high school, and government for free courses, materials, tutoring and assistance in paying for the test.

Your earning potential increases on average by another $6,000 by obtaining an associate degree. It is a much larger investment—both in time and money—but the payoff is even bigger. Community colleges are excellent resources for obtaining associate degrees economically; good community colleges will also ensure that the credits you earn will transfer if you decide to go on for your bachelor degree. The odds are that you will—we know this because we know you want to succeed and are willing to do what it takes to make that happen. Earning potential more than doubles when you obtain a bachelor degree versus not having your GED.

Education is one key to better economic prospects. But it isn't the only key. There are many people who have become successful without advanced degrees. These people understand their own personalities and talents and have found ways to put those to work for them. This is a possibility for you too. This kind of success is more attached to the controllable challenges we will discuss in the next section. To circumvent education, you will have to develop positive communication and an opportunity attitude. We will talk about this more in the "Solutions to Controllable Challenges" section later.

LEARN TO LIVE LOCAL

We cannot always dictate where we live when we arrive in America. But we can minimize the ties that keep us financially bound to Sudan. Why should we invest our hard-earned money where we can see no positive return? This is your new home country and you should plan for your life and kids *here*. Recent reports indicate that Sudan will take a very long time to return to a normal civil society; it will take decades to come before it is a comfortable place to live and raise families. Recovery is a slow process. Instead of unrealistically planning to build houses and invest in Sudan, we should do it right here in the USA.

Building community is important. The more bridges, the better: within the Sudanese community, within the black American community, and with those of other ethnicities and races. Coming to terms with the realities of our current neighborhoods is important. Some of us find ourselves suddenly among people who do not look or sound like us at all. Others of us find ourselves surrounded by other brown people but of totally different backgrounds. There are commonalities regardless. Ignorant and bias keep us from getting to know our neighbors and finding that common ground.

Specifically we Sudanese continue to see ourselves as different from black Americans. This prejudice is based on a misunderstanding that benefits those in power. It keeps us from uniting with other dispossessed and oppressed peoples to create positive change. There is an untapped power in embracing blackness. We can become part of the black American evolution in the US. All of us have been manipulated by systems that tell us we are not beautiful, we are not intelligent, we are not capable, we are not enough. Choosing to see how we are similar and how we can change these misconceptions together will add volume to our voices. In solidarity we can make a difference.

Through a focus on living locally we can have influence over the government and its programs, the school system and children's activities, the economy and job creation. When we concentrate on what is here in front of us, it becomes apparent how many opportunities there are.

Eat Well, Live Well

Some of the opportunities for a healthy, successful life here in the US we bring with us from Sudan. One of the best advantages we have for longevity is our cooking tradition. Our way of eating is much healthier and robust than the average American diet, which is filled with processed sugar and simple carbohydrates. In this way, it is healthier for us to integrate but *not* assimilate.

The garlic, peppers, and spices that are common in Sudanese food are excellent sources of the nourishment the body needs to regulate blood pressure, blood sugar, and cholesterol. This will maintain heart health and help to stave off diabetes, obesity and cancers. The leading killers.

It may be difficult at first. The cheapest foods to buy are those with the least nutritional value. This is where taking advantage of available government welfare programs can be beneficial. Applying for programs like SNAP food stamps (Supplemental Nutrition Assistance Program), WIC (Women, Infants, and Children) and other food supplement programs can help you find the funds to purchase fresh foods for you and your family. Gaining access to these fresh foods is imperative to keeping your strength and your health.

Likewise other programs can assist you in finding and affording safe housing, affordable healthcare, assistance with extra income and education. These are excellent _short-term_ resources as you get your bearings. On a federal, state and local level there are numerous organizations, charities and programs that can assist you in making ends meet until you can do so on your own. But remember that is always the goal—to make it on your own. Finding the resources that will help you obtain the shelter and food you need to stay healthy will allow you to escape becoming a statistic through early death. Using those resources to gain education and employment to become self sufficient is how you will succeed in making a full and happy life.

Living a clean, healthy lifestyle is no guarantee of a _long_ life, but it is a much better bet. The American lifestyle is seductive, glittery and glamorous—but heavy drinking, promiscuity, and drug culture are dangerous. The lure of wealth and power are equally corrupting. Without judgment, these behaviors are found on the path to prison, poverty and death. Here we must not forget our foundations in Islamic teachings and in our cultural focus on family and generosity. We are to honor ourselves, honor each other and honor our God in all things.

While Islam is a minority religion in the US, there

are many mosques and religious centers scattered all across the country. Seek out those who can assist you in maintaining your spiritual focus. This sentiment extends into the concept of the melting pot.

MELT IN THE POT

It is easy to blend in, go with the flow and accept whatever comes our way. But that is a pessimistic, reactionary approach. We are hardworking, intelligent people. We cannot allow ourselves to fall into complacent laziness. It will take work to build a respected immigrant community with a powerful voice, but we can. It will be a painful process accepting our blackness and advocating for a better life regardless of skin color, but we can. It will be a challenge to observe our religious customs in this majority Christian country, but we can. First we must accept reality. Then we can advocate for ourselves. And finally we will be empowered to promote activism within our Sudanese American community and our local communities.

Unlike the subjugation of many in Sudan, we are free to practice our religion and customs here as long as they break no laws. This is important in helping others to understand Islam and what it means to be Muslim. Radicals across the world have given us all a bad name. We have an opportunity to redefine the image of Muslims in America. This also means extending the same religious tolerance to others as we expect to enjoy. We must seek opportunities to speak with others about who we are and what we believe. Building bridges with other religious communities with similar values, if not the same faith, can bring positive growth to our community. We will not find the same respect for Islam here as we know in Sudan. However, we can increase acceptance and understanding by being true examples of our beliefs.

Likewise, we have an opportunity to help redefine the term African American. We have no association with the conflict between police and black Americans, or any direct link with the history of the healthcare system (economic, cultural) of the United States and people of color. We had no part in the American context of slavery or the perceptions of blacks that followed. But, we can have a positive impact on how black Americans are viewed today. Instead of succumbing to statistics, we can create new metrics. We cannot change the past, but we can help shape the future.

In shaping our future, we may also need to reframe our own customs. For example: In traditional Sudanese gatherings, women and men do not mix in seating. We know this is not because women are not valued but because everyone enjoys a certain freedom of comfort in this arrangement. These kinds of practices may quickly become outdated in the American context. The idea of comfort in this new context will most certainly change—as will many other things. We need to understand that not all of our practices are good or appropriate today, even if they're what we have always done. To integrate with an attitude of opportunity, we may have to let some of our old beliefs go. More about this in the next sections.

Responding to Controllable Challenges

Learn the Lingua Franca

It is important to be understood. It is an odd human reaction to assume someone dumb when they cannot easily express themselves in your language. It doesn't make sense. We know there are hundreds (maybe thousands) of living languages, but we still talk louder or slower, smile awkwardly when someone is not fluent in our language. When already facing barriers due to things you cannot control—like skin color (except through extreme means), initial economics, education, location—why make it harder on yourself?

While there is no official language in the United States, there is a historical preference to English. You may be able to get by very well at first with a limited mastery of English, but in order to extend past your immigrant neighbors and interact with the larger community, it is important to become proficient. There are many programs offered for children and adults to assist you in becoming a fluent speaker.

No, you may never fully lose your accent. But, you will gain the gift of expression. To advocate for oneself—whether it is to get a job, request a raise, run for political office, or support your children's education—you must have a voice. Learning the language of currency will encourage your chances of being heard.

This also extends to nonverbal communication. You can positively communicate through your body language and your external presentation. There are no absolute rules in the US about what to wear or how to wear it; but you will notice there are many cultural differences. Paying attention to those differences can help make the difference in your life. There are social standards for how to present yourself at a job interview—this can even vary from one field to another. There are practical standards for how to dress in different seasons (this can be a challenge in especially cold places).

Similarly, there are cultural nuances to body language and demeanor. We Sudanese tend to be shy and demure in the presence of outsiders. This may not be to our benefit. For instance, eye contact is an important part of communication. While you may naturally be shy or mild mannered, avoiding eye contact can be read as insincerity or an indication of lying. Likewise, slouching can be an indication of self-doubt or discomfort. Standing tall, looking alert and speaking up will give you the appearance of confidence and intelligence. And when you are truly in doubt, sometimes a simple smile will take you a long way.

Seek assistance to understand what is appropriate and when. Do not be afraid to ask questions. Most people genuinely want to help you, even if they don't know exactly how.

ATTEND TO ATTITUDE

A popular American saying is, "We're not in Kansas anymore, Toto." This reference to *The Wizard of Oz* simply means we aren't in our homeland anymore—we have traveled somewhere strange and new. Old notions and preconceptions will not benefit you in this new place.

Building community here may mean something a little different than before. Opportunity changes people. If you allow it, people here may surprise you, and you may surprise yourself.

We are a generous people, but so often we have not been generous with each other. There are far too few Sudanese here to continue to carry the same cultural baggage. Show empathy and respect to other

Sudanese regardless of their origin, hair or skin. All of us face similar challenges here. Internal segregation will only isolate us further. Our diversity is our strength here. Let us use it.

Encouragement is something sorely lacking in our communities. In my personal observations, we Sudanese often disagree on everything and like to argue about anything. This cannot lead to an environment of trust and support. There is enough opportunity here to go around; we need not squabble over trivial matters. There is so little time to tackle the big things, how can we waste that time on such insignificant matters?

Those of us trying to create positive change often run across the same obstacle—*naysayers*.

It is so easy to belittle the efforts and ideas of others. The hard work is actually making progress. If your mouth is busy with discouragement, your mind cannot be at the good work of creation. There is a bad habit thinking that we are the smartest person in the room and should be treated as such. If you are the smartest person in the room, then you are in the wrong room. You cannot grow if you already know everything—and if you do, then you should already have what you want. If you are like most of the rest of us, still reaching for success, then put your pride and ego in your back pocket. There is no point in being the smartest person in the room. But there is a benefit to pooling our knowledge to create a smarter, safer, more successful community.

Where others are doing something positive in the community, find ways to encourage it! For all our outward seeming generosity and warmth, we have not practiced doing good for people and we have not encouraged each other to do good. We must grow the courage to initiate something—to become the trailblazers we need. We talk about doing but we do not actually do it! Unless someone else sticks their neck out to do it—then we disparage them until we see them succeed. All of a sudden, everyone then wants to follow. This slows down our progress.

Have respect for others' ideas and roles in the community. Everyone has something to contribute. We all have talents, and they are all needed to make this community strong and prosperous. Some of our talents may be similar, but our outlooks, experiences and personalities are not—there is always something more someone else can add to build us stronger.

It is not easy to let go. But it helps to look forward. There is a temptation to yearn for an idealized past. Whatever conflicts we find here must be compared honestly with the challenges of Sudan. There is no comparison. We have to have an "opportunity attitude"—a disposition open to new experiences, new ways of behaving, new methods of operating, and new eyes through which to see our reality.

Say Farewell to Welfare

Welfare is a necessary step for many of us when we enter the country. It is *not* a life strategy. To qualify for welfare you must be single, poor and without real prospects. That is not the path to success.

Our strength is in our families. Welfare demands that families be separated, father from mother, parent from child. This is not a productive tradeoff. We *must* keep our families together, despite the temptations provided to low income and single mother status by the government. Splintering families to get free benefits creates chaos and leads to disaster in the identity creation of our children.

We need to get out of this system in order to place our children in better schools, build our lives in safer neighborhoods, and create opportunities for increased income—all of which will boost self-esteem. Weaning yourself off of assistance may be difficult to start, but it is a necessary growth process. It will pay off in the long run. The immediate benefits of welfare are many, but not enough to remain poor.

In addition, public housing is no longer something to which people aspire. The current sentiment on refugees and immigrants calls for "re-education" in public assistance and makes it difficult to get these houses. There is a massive crackdown on what some call "fake poor" specifically directed towards refugees and immigrants. Those who are poor on paper but have found the means to make money in ways that go unreported to the government.

This is another incentive for Sudanese Americans to get out of welfare. Our religious teachings prohibit believers from making a living on the basis of lies and deceit. To continue to qualify for benefits, many report false information. For instance, they conceal net income by taking jobs that are not traceable by the IRS, or claim to be single mothers while still married to, and in some cases, living with their husbands. These actions violate our core protective values. Therefore, the value of the reward is undermined by the untruthfulness.

Freebies seldom support self-independence. And none of us came here to become enslaved to the welfare system.

There are positive ways to take full and fair advantage of the system. Programs exist to help you in times of need. So use them. But when you no longer need them, get out of the way so that others in need can get to the resources. Also, be careful to use the programs that best benefit you to succeed. There are so many programs to support education at no cost to you. There are job placement programs. English language courses. Mentorship organizations. A net of support exists, but it won't come to you. It is up to you to seek it out.

The truth is that none of these programs is free. Someone pays to provide you with the opportunity for support. Once you are in a position of freedom, consider giving back to these organizations. Too often it is forgotten that real people made sacrifices for the help you receive. In order for the benefits to continue, it is up to you to pay it forward.

Responding Wrap-Up

Much of what we've discussed is about you as an individual and your journey to integration. Understanding there are some things you cannot control on a cultural level but can change on an individual level is important. There is every reason to be positive about claiming your place in the American identity. Especially, if you tackle those challenges that you can control with energy and enthusiasm. You can speak the language. You can engage with and create community. You can overcome welfare dependence. It all starts with an optimistic "opportunity attitude."

In the next section, we will discuss how to take all of the changes that you've made as an individual to benefit your children in their efforts to be successful Sudanese Americans.

CHAPTER THREE

RAISING CHILDREN IN DIASPORA

This will be difficult to understand and accept at first for many. Your children are not you. They will not have the same life outlook or experiences as you have had. They will not believe exactly as you do. You are Sudanese, but your children will be American. Even children born in Sudan will become Americanized much faster than you.

Youth have the gift of adaptability and they learn quickly through observation. They will find your stories of the old world foreign and distant. What will be real to them is the life they see every day outside their homes, in the streets, in the classroom and in their friend's homes. Things like the mall, the corner store, computers and iPods, Xboxes and cable, processed foods and microwaves will be commonplace for our kids.

Our children are American citizens and want to be raised as such. They will expect certain freedoms that would have been outrageous or out of the question for us. Their sense of values will rub up against ours and test the bounds of our morality and principles. As responsible parents, we will have to seriously consider what we believe is right and wrong and *why*. We cannot afford to naively believe our children will simply believe us. We cannot afford to naively believe our children will just listen and obey. They will not. They will not understand our ways because they will not have grown up with them. It is our responsibility to teach our children about our culture, our customs and our beliefs. But more—it is our responsibility to make this relevant to their young American lives.

This is the greatest challenge.

We must consciously plan and devote time to parenting. The stringent religious guidelines with which we were reared may not serve us well in raising our own children. Going from a country that is majority Muslim to a country majority Christian already creates an interesting and difficult difference. Then add this different dynamic: going from a nation that is majority brown to one majority white. And another crucial difference: going from an unstable virtually authoritarian government to a stable democracy (flawed though it may be). Americans exaggerate about the warzones of the inner city, but we Sudanese understand what it is to come from a war-torn country. We know what it is to see millions of your countrymen murdered. This is a reality that our children are likely never to know in the United States.

Consciously devoting time to parenting and family planning starts with understanding these differences in our own minds. There are beliefs that we held to survive. Now we need to assess all of those beliefs and decide what is needed to thrive in our new lives.

How are *we* as parents adapting?

What are *reasonable* expectations of our children?

What standards can we let go?

What principles are steadfast and always relevant? When we can answer these questions for ourselves, then we need to be able to *communicate* them to our children.

Childrearing Challenges

Communication

Kids speak a different language. This is always true of youth. They have their own slang and style. But now this slang and style is influenced by a new country with its own cultures. The United States is founded on the belief that every person has the right to their own life, liberty and pursuit of happiness. People are encouraged to be individuals and to express themselves. Difference is celebrated. But that celebration can lead to headaches in your household.

Everything outside of your home will encourage your kids to question you at best, and disregard your opinions at worst. These factors may seem to build a wall between you and your children. This wall can lead to a break down in the relationship. Without a trusting, open relationship between children and parents, kids may not open up to parents with their problems—until it is too late. Several factors may hinder your ability to communicate with your children. These are a few of the most important:

TRADITION

We parents tend to want to raise our kids the same way we were raised. We have a certain tradition of parental dictatorship and child obedience. We expect our children to learn and understand responsibility early in life—mostly through doing as we say.

Likewise, we expect our children to share our moral and religious values. We shove children into Islamic practices without clear explanation of purpose. We have too many spiritual and religious expectations of our children in a country that does not generally reflect our beliefs. This may cause confusion and intensify rebellious behavior.

Our children see options. They will want to understand why Islam is important to us and why they should believe as we do when so many others around us do not. They will want to understand why they should continue our customs and culture when Sudan for them is so far away. They will want to know why they should listen to us when we are not succeeding ourselves.

ISOLATION

Because we fear our children being corrupted, we parents may lean toward isolation. It is natural for likeminded people to gather together. As newcomers to the US, often we settle in communities of other Sudanese. Then we pay no particular attention to active integration. We discourage our children from mingling with others (non-Sudanese) to minimize their influence. But this is impossible. In order for our children to be successful they must have relationships with other people—especially those who are different. More importantly, they will *want* to have relationships with those outside of our Sudanese immigrant community.

Our traditions will not be our children's traditions. Their community will not only be Sudanese, but American.

TIME

Time is a luxury that so many of us do not have. We all face many hardships that eat away at our time. Work is the most common problem. But it is a part of life. We must work to have or do just about anything else, including the basics—food, clothing, shelter. While there are many opportunities in the United States, work is still difficult. Getting good work is hard. Keeping good work is hard. We spend so much of our lives at work, sometimes we become strangers to the people we live with at home.

This is where time affects our children.

We parents are so busy trying to monetarily support our families that we sometimes forget to emotionally and physically support each other with our time. There is nothing more important to our kids than spending time with us. And not only do children need time, but our *spouses* need our time too. They need us to just be there.

Being there for your family is more than just bringing home a pay check. It is being there physically, emotionally and mentally. They need us to talk to them, but more importantly to listen to them. They need us to show up for their important moments and be present in mind and body. They need us to support their dreams and help them battle their fears.

Yes, it is hard to balance the financial responsibility with the emotional needs of family. Time is a finite resource—we can't go out and make more. But that's why it so precious. That's why it's the most important thing you can give to your family. It is the one thing more than any other that will build bonds of trust and hope.

EDUCATION

I have seen it. Parents are not paying attention to their children's education. Too often restrictions on time make it such that parents don't know what children do in school—or if children are in school at all. We mostly rely on the system to take care of our children's education. This is a dangerous practice. The school system is only meant to do so much, and the rest is up to us. The schools our children go to are only as good as the parents who support them (Figure 5).

I know it's not that we don't care. There are barriers that keep us from supporting our children: lack of education ourselves, lack of time, and lack of language skills.

Lack of education: At a certain point for many of us, our children will surpass our own education. It can be difficult and embarrassing trying to keep up. It's sometimes easier to just get out of the way.

Lack of time: Working to make sure our children have what they need, and trying to better ourselves takes up a lot of time. The average work week is supposed to be 40 hours, but we all know that many of us easily work double that.

Lack of Language Skills: The United States doesn't have an official language—but if it did, it would be English. The majority of people speak English. And the majority of schools teach all subjects in English. Not being proficient in English makes it difficult to interact with teachers and administrators. It also makes it difficult to be involved with your children's educational experience.

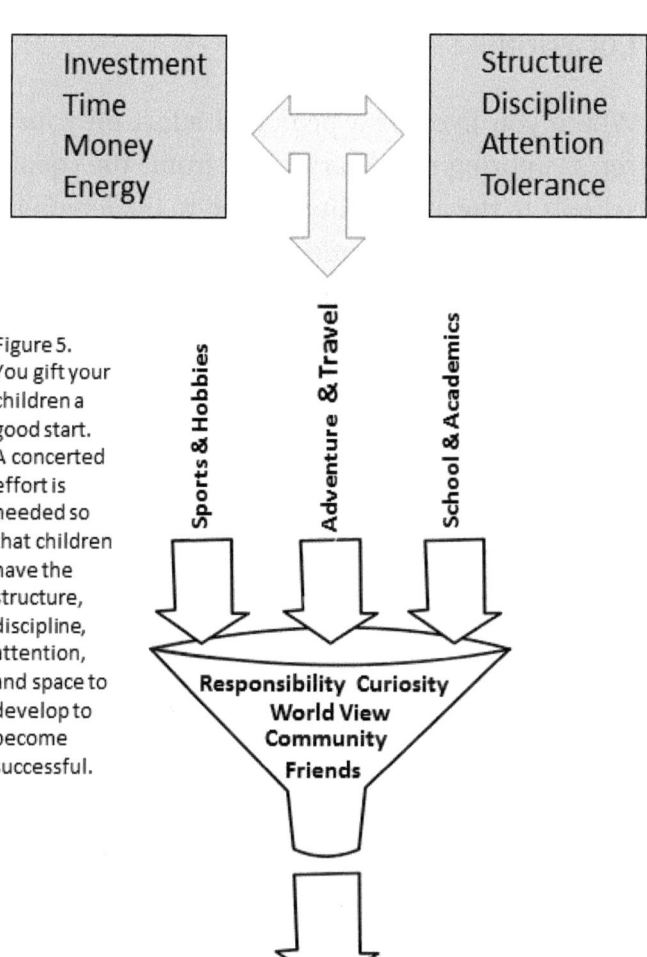

Figure 5. You gift your children a good start. A concerted effort is needed so that children have the structure, discipline, attention, and space to develop to become successful.

Location

Where you live has a profound effect on your children's upbringing. Everything from the quality of schools to the availability of food to the length of your commute to work is affected by your zip code. Environment plays a large part in how your children interact with and understand the world. Healthy bodies, relationships and mindsets can be compromised by an unhealthy living situation.

The inner city is fraught with challenges like gang activity, high incidents of early school dropouts, overcrowding, and neighborhood segregation by income. Suburban environments have their own issues: Relations may be strained by friction as immigrants disturb the existing structures and norms. Incidents of hate crimes and segregation by race and income have increased as immigrant populations have increased.

In addition, there are certain things that location will not shield our children from. Sex, drugs, alcohol and other illicit and illegal things are readily available if given the time and opportunity to find them. When kids are left to their own devices, they will find trouble. That trouble comes in various shapes, sizes and consequences no matter where you live.

Sometimes we have little choice in the matter of location. We live where we can afford to live. Even when we can afford to live in places deemed "better" or "good" that doesn't eliminate potential problems. If we aren't paying attention to how our location is affecting our children, we won't understand who our children are becoming.

CHILDREARING COMEBACK

TALK THE TALK, WALK THE WALK

Your kids don't expect you to speak the same way they do. They'd probably be embarrassed if you tried. But they do expect honesty from their parents. Children do hope for acceptance from their parents. They do want to be in communication with you, no matter how often they seem to ignore you. This is probably even truer when children feel isolated and alone. They need you to listen to them without fear of judgment. Children are trying just as hard as you are to make a way for themselves in this very confusing world. They will be going through many changes and challenges the same way you are, but with none of your life experience and wisdom. If you engage your children openly and honestly, they will trust that they can communicate with you the same way.

It is tempting to adopt a "Do as I say, not as I do" attitude. But it is also dangerous. When our children see us contradicting ourselves they lose confidence in us. When our children see us engaging in inappropriate or inadvisable behavior, it is difficult for them to properly adjust their own moral compass. That is why we must talk the talk and walk the walk. If we want our kids to be morally upstanding citizens, then we must model that for them. If we want our kids to talk to us when they have problems, we must create a safe space in which they can come to us.

We have to make time for them.

When you engage your children where they are, instead of expecting them to be where you are, you will find that the wall between you crumbles away. That is not to say that we must accept their nonsense or excuses or inappropriate behavior. No. But we should make room to hear their thoughts, allow them to speak their dreams, encourage them to be successful individuals in their own right—not demand they be mirror images of ourselves.

Create Cultural Connection

One way we can support our kids' success is by introducing them to our heritage. We must convey the value in our culture. The things that we think are normal and expected will not be so normal to our kids. We have to be the bridge between our kids' new American way of life and the old Sudanese ways.

We must share our customs with our children in fun ways. When there are no demands and expectations, it becomes a choice, instead of a chore, for our children to engage in our traditions. There are also many parallels between our celebrations and those that we will find in the US. We should become more knowledgeable about these similarities to stimulate our children's involvement and interest.

We must always keep in touch with our families in Sudan. We should take our children to our homeland whenever possible. Our culture is beautiful and we must tell them our stories. They will understand more who they are, when they see who we are and from where we have come. They will also learn to appreciate what they have when they see how different life is in Sudan. One day they will be able to tell their own stories to their own children.

How we speak defines how we think, and how we think defines our world. We must speak to each other and our children in our native tongues. We should encourage our kids to learn as many languages as possible. Language is the key to culture. Speaking more than one language helps expand the way we think. It also connects us with other people. Through our languages we can build bridges to the past and to other people around the world.

APPLY FOR WORLD CITIZENSHIP

As we are building bridges between our children and

our homeland, why not make one more leap? While we create connection to our roots, we should also promote diversity and acceptance to our children. Exposure to various cultures will expand their vision and increase their understanding of the world. Get them excited to see the world! As you can, give your kids the gift of travel.

Domestic and international, near and far, by car and by plane, by boat and by train. These experiences will help mold their character. Travel pushes you beyond your comfort zone. You are forced to engage with new people and discover new things. Travel builds confidence and allows the brain to be more flexible. Learning new languages and ways of operating in the world, youth are exposed to more possibilities. Travel builds cultural sensitivity and awareness that there are many different kinds of people in the world. When you see how many ways you can live and interact with each other and the earth, your understanding of life and opportunity changes.

You immigrated to give your family more opportunity. Encouraging travel only increases your kids' awareness of opportunity and options.

Stir Them in the Pot

You cannot take advantage of opportunity in a bubble. Instead of isolating our children from their new country, we need to introduce them to it wholeheartedly. This way we can control what they are engaged in and how.

Get the kids involved in sports, music and other intellectually challenging activities. There are activities available through their schools, local colleges, and community groups for kids with every interest: computers and technology, sports and fitness, strategy and tactics, creative and artistic, individual or social—you name it. Introduce them to nature; take them fishing and camping. Keep them busy with activities. The more active with positive outlets, the better. Help your children identify their interests and support them in finding both individual and team or group applications for those interests. Encourage them to exercise both their minds and their bodies.

Also remember to let them rest. Don't be grumpy if your teenager seems to sleep all day. Sleep is important for proper growth and optimal attention. Let them get as much sleep as possible. But when they are awake, push them to find interesting people, places and things to become involved with.

Support your children in making good friends. Connecting with their peers is very important in your child's development. By being involved with their friend groups, you can ensure they have a responsible adult around whom they can trust. This is important for your kids *and* their friends. You will be creating a circle of positivity. Try to set up play dates, organize activities, and support social interaction. This will demonstrate to your children how important healthy relationships and positive connections are. Try to remember their friends' birthdays and important events: it makes your children feel special, because you are acknowledging important people in their lives; *and* it makes their friends feel special, because you are a committed member of their community.

Help them to engage in the community through outreach and charity work. Volunteering is an excellent way to build their moral character; it is a moral obligation to give back and help those less fortunate. In addition to this, volunteering will help your kids network with influential people and start to build their own resumes. It will also give them a greater understanding of their environment.

Teens who volunteer are also less likely to use drugs or become pregnant; and they are more likely to have positive academic, psychological, and occupational well-being. Adolescents who are involved in community service or who volunteer in political activities are more likely as adults to have a strong work ethic, to volunteer, and to vote. Volunteering is also associated with the development of greater respect for others, leadership skills, and an understanding of citizenship that can carry over into adulthood.

Be with and support them, and share your experiences and your own stories. Help them to see how *you* add flavor to the big melting pot of their environment.

EDUCATE YOURSELF ON EDUCATION

We must shift our mental model with our kids and raise them as individuals capable of surviving and succeeding in Western culture. Without our guidance and support, our teenagers are getting into trouble and dropping out of school. We must make the effort to ensure all of our hardship is worth it, protecting their lives and their interests.

First, we discussed earlier the importance of bettering ourselves with higher education. This step will make it that much easier for you to support your own children as they progress through school.

Second, make an effort to enroll your children in the best schools possible. Sometimes you don't have a lot of choices, but try to do a little research to see what options you do have. Sometimes moving just one block over can change your child's school district and drastically improve the resources available to them.

Last, you can ensure your kids are in a good school by showing your face regularly: Go to the school just to check up on your child and check in with their teachers. Attend all of your kid's school activities. Go to the school meetings and get involved with the Parent–Teacher organization.

It may not be fair, but it's true: The squeaky wheel gets the oil. School teachers generally pay better attention to kids whose parents actively show interest in their children's education. So make the effort to pay just a little bit more attention.

Rearing Wrap-Up

Children over time are meant to claim independence from their parents. This is part of growing into adulthood. In order to be a successful adult—to work, earn a living, build a family—children must eventually come from under their parents protective wings and learn to fend for themselves.

To support them in doing this, you do not have to be perfect; you just have to be there.

That's the real point of this entire section. We want to encourage you to be there for your children to enable them to build their own identity and integrate into the American social fabric.

CONCLUSION

REMOVING THE SPLINTER

THE INDIVIDUAL SOUL

According to Susan Pinker, a developmental psychologist, social integration may be the most important factor in a long life. Not exercise or modern medicine. Not a healthy lifestyle or environmental factors. Your *social life* might be the secret to living longer. Whether or not you build strong bonds with people where you set down your roots is an incredible indicator of the quality of life you will have.

I want to challenge you to commit to rooting yourself here in the US. To creating community here. While I would never suggest you give up your Sudanese identity, I would encourage you to invest in your American life. We spend money investing in and building homes in Sudan when we know there is little hope that we will return in the near future. I challenge you to loosen your attachment to the nostalgic past and instead make room for a successful integrated future here in America.

Our children need us to commit. We made a choice to build our families here and they need us to succeed. We must embrace those different from us to gain power, friendship, trust, loyalty, and relationships. We can harness these differences to better our community. "People who are not like us make us grow" (Rabbi Jonathan Sacks).

Despite the extreme challenges of being in a different place, different culture and out of the comfort or our homeland, it is entirely possible to be happy, raise children and lead a successful gratifying life.

THE SOUL OF THE PEOPLE

It is critically important that people from third world and sub-Saharan Africa remember that Western nations are bonding together to prevent the migration influx of people who look like us into their countries. Those few who are allowed to enter Western countries legally are marginalized and kept at bay from the main economic stream. They realize that there is a cultural revolution in the making. If this influx were left alone, 100 years from today there would be no white persons anymore. People of all colors are coming together to redefine the rainbow of humanity—and whiteness is being phased out. For this reason, we see that immigration reforms are taking center-stage in presidential debates, all levels of election cycles and policy making.

The hard truth is that the West has no genuine interest in resolving African problems. The evidence is clear in the international response to crises. For Darfur, Rwanda, Somalia, and the Congo, the international outcry was lethargic at best, but best described as critically negligent. Close to three-fourths of the world is suffering from acute injustice. And the West benefits from the genocide, standing aside as Africans kill each other.

As a people we must take responsibility because we collectively share our destiny and future. These times call for a way of life shift to overcome the problems that have plagued Sudan, and other areas of the African diaspora. We must stop talking about "I," "me," and "self" and replace it with "we" and "us." It is not enough to send money back home to family. The stakes are too great and the consequences too dire for us to continue to look at this only as individuals. There are many people in our communities and villages in Sudan who are not able to survive without intervention. No one is going to save us but ourselves. But we *cannot* do the work when we are so *divided*.

Here we have the opportunity to redefine ourselves and our relationship to each other and our homeland Sudan. Here we have the opportunity to grow as individuals and as a united force. Here we have the opportunity to stitch the wounds of division and heal the splintered souls of our people. When we embrace the wholeness of who we are, we are beautiful.

We are black Americans of Sudanese descendent.

BIBLIOGRAPHY

BlackPast.org. "African American History Timeline." http://www.blackpast.org/african-american-history-timeline-home-page

Bushara, Mohamed N. 2008. Odd Racism & Tribalism Have Halted Sudan's Prosperity, www.frontline resourcesblog.com

Bushara, Mohamed N. 2007. Yet Another Africans Challenge: Liability No. 21 The IQ. http://sudaneseonline. com/board/12/msg/Yet-Another-Africans-Challenge%3A-Liability-No.-21-the-IQ-By-Dr.-Mohamed-N.-Bushara*-1195138888.htm

Cella, Matthew and Alan Neuhauser. September 2016. "Race and Homicide in America, by the Numbers." US News. https://www.usnews.com/news/articles/2016-09-29/race-and-homicide-in-america-by-the-numbers

Centers for Disease Control and Prevention (CDC). 2017. "Health of Black or African American non-Hispanic Population." FastStats. https://www.cdc.gov/nchs/fastats/black-health.htm

Central Intelligence Agency (CIA). 2017. "Sudan." The

World Fact Book. https:// www. cia. gov/library/ publications/the-world-factbook/geos/su.html

Chanda, Chisala. 2015. "The IQ Gap Is No Longer A Black And White Issue, Comments& Reply, The Unz Review: An Alternative Media Selection," Http://www.unzcom/article/The-Iq-Gap-Is-No-Longer-A-Black-And-White-Issue/

ChildTrends. 2015. "Volunteering." https://www.childtrends.org/indicators/volunteering/

Hashim, Mohammed Jalal A. 2007. "The Arabization of Sudan." African Writing Online, June-August. http://www.african-writing.com/aug/jalal.htm

Herrnstein, Richard & Charles Murray. 1994. *The Bell Curve*.

History.com. 2009. "Slavery in America." http://www.history.com/topics/black-history/slavery

Institute on Assets and Social Policy (IASP), Brandeis University. 2017. The Asset Value of Whiteness: Understanding the Racial Wealth Gap http://iasp.brandeis. edu/pdfs/2017/AssetValue.pdf

Johnson, Oscar. "Chilly Coexistence: Africans and African Americans in the Bronx" http://www.columbia.edu/itc/journalism/gissler/anthology/Chill-Johnson.html

Limbaugh, Rush. 1992. The Way Things Ought to Be

NAACP. 2018. "Criminal Justice Fact Sheet." www.naacp.org/criminal-justice-fact-sheet

Pinker, Susan. April 2017. "The Secret to Living Longer May Be Your Social Life." https://www.ted.com/talks/susan_pinker_the_secret_to_living_longer_may_be_your_social_life#t-53928

Sacks, Jonathan. July 2017. "How We Can Face the Future without Fear, Together." Ted talk.

Sudanese American Medical Association (SAMA), "SAMA Chicago Health Fair, May 27th Monday 2013" Report provided by SAMA

U.S. Census Bureau. 2017. Profile America Facts for Features: CB17-FF.01. www.census.gov/newsroom/facts-for-features/2017/cb17-ff01.html

U.S. Department of Education, National Center for Education Statistics. 2017. Common Core of Data, America's Public Schools, "Table 1. Public high school 4-year adjusted cohort graduation rate (ACGR), 2015–16." https://nces.ed.gov/ccd/tables/ACGR_RE_and_characteristics_2015-16.asp

U.S. Department of Education, National Center for Education Statistics. 2017. The Condition of Education 2017 (NCES 2017-144), Status Dropout Rates. https://nces.ed.gov/fastfacts/display.asp?id=16

U.S. Department of Health and Human Services, Centers for Disease Control and Prevention, National Center for Health Statistics. *National Vital Statis-*

tics Reports 66:1. https://www.cdc.gov/nchs/data/nvsr/nvsr66/nvsr66_01.pdf

Williams, David R. "How Racism Makes Us Sick," Ted talk, Posted Apr 2017

Wallach, Ari. 2015. "Sandbag Strategy: 3 Ways to Plan for the (Very) Long Term." Ted talk.

Wikipedia. 2017. "Islam in the United States." https://en.wikipedia.org/wiki/Islam_in_the_United_States

Wikipedia. 2017. "Slavery in Sudan." https://en.wikipedia.org/wiki/Slavery_in_Sudan

Printed by Libri Plureos GmbH in Hamburg, Germany